ADAM HAMILTON

THE
CALL

THE LIFE AND MESSAGE OF
THE APOSTLE PAUL

Children's Leader Guide

by Sally Hoelscher

Abingdon Press
Nashville

THE CALL
The Life and Message of the Apostle Paul

Children's Leader Guide
by Sally Hoelscher

This book is printed on elemental chlorine-free paper.

ISBN 978-1-63088-270-9

Scripture quotations unless noted otherwise are from the Common English Bible. Copyright © 2011 by the Common English Bible. All rights reserved. Used by permission. www.CommonEnglishBible.com.

15 16 17 18 19 20 21 22 23 24—10 9 8 7 6 5 4 3 2 1

MANUFACTURED IN THE UNITED STATES OF AMERICA

Contents

To the Leader

This children's leader guide is designed for use with Adam Hamilton's book and study *The Call: The Life and Message of the Apostle Paul*. This guide includes six lessons that take a look at the life of the Apostle Paul and his message. Children will learn about Paul's life and ministry and explore God's call in their own lives.

The lessons in this guide, designed for children in kindergarten through sixth grade, are presented in a large-group/small-group format. Children begin with time spent at activity centers, followed by time together as a large group. Children end the lesson in small groups determined by age. Each lesson plan contains the following sections:

Focus for the Teacher

The information in this section will provide you with background information about the week's lesson. Use this section for your own study as you prepare.

Explore Interest Groups

Ideas for a variety of activity centers will be found in this section. These activities will prepare the children to hear the Bible story. Allow the children to choose one or more of the activities that interest them. Occasionally there will be an activity that is recommended for all children, usually because it relates directly to a later activity. When this is the case, it will be noted in the sidebar notes.

Large Group

The children will come together as a large group to hear the story for the week. This section begins with a transition activity followed by the story and a Bible verse activity. A worship time concludes the large group time.

Small Groups

Children are divided into age-level groups for small-group time. Depending on the size of your class, you may need to have more than one group for each age level. It is recommended that each small group contain no more than ten children.

Younger Children

The activities in this section are designed for children in kindergarten through second grade.

Older Children

The activities in this section are designed for children in third through sixth grades.

Reproducible Pages

At the end of each lesson are reproducible pages, to be photocopied and handed out for all the children to use during that lesson's activities.

Schedule

Many churches have weeknight programs that include an evening meal, an intergenerational gathering time, and classes for children, youth, and adults. The following schedule illustrates one way to organize a weeknight program.

5:30	Meal
6:00	Intergenerational gathering introducing weekly themes and places for the lesson. This time may include presentations, skits, music, and opening or closing prayers.
6:15–8:15	Classes for children, youth, and adults.

Churches may want to do this study as a Sunday school program. This setting would be similar to the weeknight setting. The following schedule takes into account a shorter class time, which is the norm for Sunday morning programs.

10 minutes	Intergenerational gathering
45 minutes	Classes for children, youth, and adults

Choose a schedule that works best for your congregation and its Christian education programs.

Blessings to you and the children as you learn about the life and message of the Apostle Paul!

1 Called to Follow Christ

Objectives

The children will
- hear Acts 9.
- learn about Paul's conversion experience.
- discover that God called Paul to spread the good news.
- explore how God's call may be heard in their lives.

Bible Story

Paul's Call: Acts 9

Bible Verse

God had set me apart from birth and called me through his grace. (Galatians 1:15)

Focus for the Teacher

Though born in Tarsus, a major center for Greek education and culture, Paul was a Jew and had studied in Jerusalem with Gamaliel, a leading teacher of the Law of Moses. Paul was training to be a Pharisee. The Pharisees were a group of Jewish leaders who believed that the best way to serve God was to strictly obey the Law of Moses. Prior to his conversion, Paul was often known by his Hebrew name, Saul. After his conversion, Paul used his Greek name, perhaps to signify the change that had occurred in his life.

> God called Paul for a special task.

Paul's strong beliefs as a Pharisee resulted in his determination to make trouble for the followers of Jesus. Paul is mentioned in Acts (7:58–8:1) as being present at, and approving of, the stoning of the Apostle Stephen. Following this event, Paul continued to threaten to kill the Lord's followers. It was this intent that led Paul, armed with letters to the leaders of the synagogues, to travel to Damascus to arrest Jesus' followers and take them back to Jerusalem.

As Paul traveled to Damascus, his actions were consistent with his beliefs at the time. He knew what he believed, and he was determined to follow through. On the way to Damascus, Paul had an encounter that changed his life: he met Jesus. Paul was blinded by the encounter. Paul was led into Damascus by others—not the entry into Damascus he had planned! As a result of his meeting with the risen Christ, Paul was changed, not immediately, but over time. Paul ultimately showed the same determination in recruiting followers of Jesus as he had previously shown in persecuting those followers.

Paul's conversion story is an example of God's ability to use anybody to carry out God's work. With his history of persecuting Christians, Paul seemed an unlikely candidate to spread God's word. When Ananias, a follower of Jesus, received instructions to go and talk to Paul, he questioned this direction, saying, "Lord, I have heard many reports about this man. People say he has done horrible things to your holy people in Jerusalem" (Acts 9:13). But God had a plan to use Paul to spread the news of Jesus. God called Paul for a special task and was able to use Paul's zeal and determination in a positive way. Prior to his encounter with Jesus, Paul had been living out his early beliefs; after his encounter, Paul lived out his belief in God and shared the news of Jesus' love with others.

Explore Interest Groups

Be sure that adult leaders are waiting when the first child arrives. Greet and welcome the children. Get them involved in an activity that interests them and introduces the theme for the day's activities.

Spot the Changes

- **Say:** There are some things in our classroom that look different than they usually do.

- Have the children partner up and give each pair of children a piece of paper and a pencil.

- Encourage the children to work together to list as many changes as they can find.

- Have the children compare lists to see how they did.

- **Say:** In our Bible story today we are going to be talking about change.

Prepare

✓ Prior to class, make ten to twelve changes in your classroom space. For example, you might move the location of the trash can, move a table to a different spot in the room, hang the clock upside down, and so forth.

✓ Supply pencils and paper.

Trick Your Eyes

- **Say:** Your eyes are incredible. They allow you to see many different colors. Today you are going to trick your eyes.

- Give each child a piece of white paper.

- Have the children fold the paper in half by bringing the long edges together to create a double thickness.

- Invite children to choose a red, orange, yellow, green, blue, or purple marker and use it to draw and color in a circle about the size of a quarter on the paper.

- Have each child use a black marker to put a small dot in the center of the circle.

- Encourage each child to stare at the black dot for fifteen to twenty seconds and then look at the white paper slightly to the side of the original circle.

- **Ask:** Did you see another circle? (If the answer is no, have the child concentrate on looking right at the black dot.) What color was the second circle? (See Note under Prepare.)

- **Say:** The back of your eye contains certain areas called cones that are sensitive to particular colors. White is a combination of all colors, so when you see white it means all the cones are receiving information. When you stare at one color for a long time, the cones receiving input from that color become tired and take a break. So when you stare at

Prepare

✓ Supply markers and white paper.

✓ *Tip*: Adequate lighting helps this activity work well.

✓ *Note*: The table below shows the color of the afterimage produced by each color.

Original Color	Afterimage Color
red	blue or bluish green
orange	blue
yellow	blue or bluish purple
green	reddish blue or pink
blue	yellow
purple	yellow or yellow-green

the white paper, instead of seeing white you see color from the cones that are still working.

- Invite children to try this experiment with circles containing more than one color, such as a circle that is half red and half blue.

- **Say:** We rely on our eyes for a lot of information. In our Bible story today, we will hear about a man named Paul who temporarily lost the use of his eyes. That experience changed Paul's life.

Prepare

✓ Set up a short obstacle course using objects in the room. For example, you might set up several chairs that the children have to walk around, followed by a couple of Hula-hoops lying on the floor that have to be stepped in, followed by a table that must be crawled under. It is not necessary to make the course too difficult since the children will be blindfolded.

✓ Supply blindfolds.

Blindfolded Obstacle Course

- Explain the route through the obstacle course to the children.

- Divide the children into pairs. Give each pair of children a blindfold. Have each pair decide which child will be blindfolded first.

- Invite children to lead their blindfolded partners through the obstacle course.

- Encourage the children to give verbal instructions and to lead their partner by the hand as necessary.

- After all the blindfolded children have had a chance to be led through the obstacle course, have the children switch roles.

- **Ask:** How did it feel to trust your partner to lead you through the obstacle course?

- **Say:** In our Bible story today, we will hear about a time that the Apostle Paul was temporarily blinded. Paul liked to be in control, but when he couldn't see he had to rely on other people to lead him.

Prepare

✓ Provide copies of **Reproducible 1a: Listening for God's Call**.

✓ Supply pencils.

✓ *Answers:* Bible, prayer, worship, family, friends, nature, silence

Unscramble the Words

- Give each child a pencil and a copy of Reproducible 1a: Listening for God's Call.

- Read the information at the top of the page to the children.

- Encourage children to work together or individually to unscramble the words.

Large Group

Bring all the children together to experience the Bible story. Use a bell to alert the children to the large-group time.

Lights On, Lights Off

- **Say:** It is time to move to our large-group area for our Bible story. Today we are going to move there in a fun way. When I tell you to begin, I would like you to begin walking toward our large-group area. But when I turn off the lights, you must freeze where you are. When the lights are on you may walk, but when the lights are off you need to remain where you are. When you reach our Bible story area, you may sit down.

- Play this game until all children are gathered in the large-group area.

Prepare

- ✓ *Tip:* If you do not have a separate area for large-group time, you may designate a distance the children must cross, such as from one side of the room to the other.

Paul's Call

- **Say:** The Bible stories we will hear during this study about Paul are all found in the Book of Acts, also called the Acts of the Apostles.

- **Ask:** Who were the apostles? (followers of Jesus) Do we find stories of Jesus' followers in the Old Testament or the New Testament? (New)

- **Say:** Acts is the fifth book of the New Testament. We find it right after the four Gospels, Matthew, Mark, Luke, and John.

- Have the children find Acts in their Bibles.

- **Say:** Today Paul is going to tell us his story.

- Read the story from Reproducible 1b: Paul's Call.

- Turn off the lights or close shades to make the room darker when you read about Paul becoming blind. Turn the lights back on when Paul is able to see again.

- **Ask:** Where was Paul traveling? (to Damascus) Why? (to arrest followers of Jesus) Who did Paul meet on the way? (Jesus) What happened? (Paul became blind) What did God want Paul to do? (tell other people about Jesus)

- **Say:** After he met Jesus on the road to Damascus, Paul made a major change in his life. Before he met Jesus, he was hurting Jesus' followers. After Paul regained his sight, he began encouraging people to follow Jesus—the exact opposite of what he had been doing before.

- **Ask:** Do you think it was easy for Jesus' followers to trust Paul and believe that he had changed? (probably not)

- **Say:** It was probably difficult for Jesus' followers to believe Paul had truly changed. The Bible tells us it took quite a while for Paul to gain their trust. What they learned and what we need to remember is that Jesus can change anyone's life—even Paul's!

Prepare

- ✓ Provide copies of **Reproducible 1b: Paul's Call**.

- ✓ Supply Bibles.

- ✓ Consider inviting a visitor to come and read Paul's story to the class each week of this study.

Called to Follow Christ

Prepare

✓ Write the week's Bible verse on a marker board or a piece of mural paper and place it where it can easily be seen. ("God had set me apart from birth and called me through his grace." Galatians 1:15)

Disappearing Bible Verse

- **Say:** After Paul began following Jesus, he traveled many places. We will hear about Paul's journeys in the upcoming weeks. During his travels, Paul helped start many new churches. Paul wrote letters while he was traveling. Many of his letters were written to the people in the churches he had helped start. Some of Paul's letters are in the Bible. Our Bible verses during this study are from Paul's letters. Today's verse is from a letter Paul wrote to Christians living in the region of Galatia.

- Show the children the Bible verse.

- Invite the children to read the verse with you.

- **Say:** Remember that this verse is from a letter Paul wrote, so it is Paul saying God called him.

- **Ask:** What did God call Paul to do? (spread the news about Jesus)

- Erase or cover up the words "God had."

- **Say:** Our Bible verse is disappearing, but let's see if we can still say it.

- Invite the children to say the verse with you again.

- Continue erasing or covering up two words at a time and saying the verse together until there are no words left on the marker board.

Called to Follow Christ

- Have the children close their eyes.

- **Say:** Before Paul met Jesus he didn't understand that Jesus was God's son. It was as if he were living in the dark and couldn't see the way things were.

- Have the children open their eyes.

- **Say:** Then on the way to Damascus, Paul saw a bright light and Jesus spoke to him.

- Have the children close their eyes again.

- **Say:** After meeting Jesus, Paul was blind for three days. He couldn't see anything.

- Have the children open their eyes.

- **Say:** When Paul could see again, he changed the way he lived his life. Paul realized God was calling him to follow Jesus' example about how to live and to tell others about Jesus. God calls us to follow Jesus too.

- Have the children close their eyes again.

- **Say:** As you are sitting with your eyes closed, say a silent prayer to God. As you pray, think about something you can do in the coming week to share God's love with someone else. I will close our time of silent prayer with a spoken prayer.

- Allow some time for the children to pray in silence.

- **Pray:** God, we thank you for calling us to follow Jesus. Help us to live our lives so that others will know of your love. Amen.

- Have the children open their eyes.

- Dismiss children to their small groups.

Small Groups

Divide the children into small groups. You may organize the groups around age levels or around readers and nonreaders. Keep the groups small, with a maximum of ten children in each group. You may need to have more than one group of each age level.

Young Children (Ages 5-7)

- Invite children to draw pictures of themselves.

- Have the following discussion while children are drawing.

- **Say:** Today we heard a story about the Apostle Paul.

- **Ask:** How did Paul change in the Bible story today? (He began to believe in and follow Jesus.) Did Paul look different when he began following Jesus? (No)

- **Say:** Paul looked the same on the outside, but Paul had changed on the inside. You have changed a lot from the time you were born until now.

- **Ask:** How have you changed on the outside from the time you were born until now?

- Allow the children time to offer their ideas.

- **Say:** You have also changed in many ways that cannot be seen. One example might be learning to write your name. I cannot tell by looking at you that you know how to write your name.

- **Ask:** How have you changed in ways that cannot be seen from the time you were born until now?

- Allow the children time to offer their ideas.

- **Say:** When we follow Jesus, it doesn't change the way we look, just like it didn't change the way Paul looked. But following Jesus did change the way Paul acted!

- **Ask:** How does believing in Jesus change us on the inside? How does following Jesus change the way we act?

- Allow the children time to offer their ideas.

- **Say:** When we believe Jesus is God's son, we want to follow the example he showed us about the way to live our lives.

- Have the children cover their eyes with their hands, remembering that Paul couldn't see for three days after encountering Jesus.

- **Pray:** God of change, we give thanks for the many ways we have changed since we were born. We hear you calling us to follow Jesus. Help us remember that following Jesus changes the way we treat other people. Amen.

- Have the children uncover their eyes.

Prepare

✓ Supply paper and crayons.

Prepare

✓ Provide paper and pencils.

Older Children (Ages 8–11)

- **Say:** Today we have heard a story about the Apostle Paul making a change. We are going to continue talking about change and talk about the difference between outside changes and inside changes.

- **Ask:** How did Paul change in the Bible story today? (He began to believe in and follow Jesus.) Did Paul's appearance change when he began following Jesus? (No, the change was on the inside.)

- Give each child a piece of paper and a pencil.

- Have each child fold the paper in half, bringing the short sides together.

- **Say:** You have changed a lot from the time you were born until now. Some of those changes can be noticed when someone looks at you.

- Invite children to write down on the outside of their folded paper ways they have changed on the outside from the time they were born until now.

- Give the children time to write.

- Encourage children to share what they have written with each other.

- Have the children open their papers up to the inside.

- **Say:** You have also changed in many ways that cannot be seen by looking at you. One example is learning to read. I cannot tell by looking at you whether you know how to read.

- Invite children to write down on the inside of their paper ways they have changed on the inside from the time they were born until now.

- Give the children time to write.

- Encourage children to share what they have written with each other.

- **Say:** When we follow Jesus, it doesn't change the way we look, just like it didn't change the way Paul looked. But following Jesus did change the way Paul acted!

- **Ask:** How does believing in Jesus change us on the inside? How does following Jesus change the way we act?

- **Say:** Paul was called to follow Jesus, and so are we. If we answer the call to follow Jesus it will change our lives.

- Have the children cover their eyes with their hands, remembering that Paul couldn't see for three days after encountering Jesus.

- **Pray:** God of change, we give thanks for the many ways we have changed during our lives, on the outside and the inside. We hear you calling us to follow Jesus. Help us remember that following Jesus changes the way we treat other people. Help us look for opportunities to share your love and do your work. Amen.

- Have the children uncover their eyes.

Listening for God's Call

The Bible contains many stories about God calling people to do God's work. One time God spoke from a burning bush. Another time Jesus spoke to a man traveling from Jerusalem to Damascus. Although we may not experience God speaking to us from a burning bush or hear Jesus speaking to us, God does call us to do God's work in the world. Unscramble the words below to discover some places where we might hear, see, and understand God's call for our lives.

BLIEB   — — — — —

PARERY   — — — — — —

PWHOISR   — — — — — — —

YMLFIA   — — — — — —

DEFINRS   — — — — — — —

TURNAE   — — — — — —

ECNLISE   — — — — — — —

Can you think of other ways you might discover what God wants you to do?

What do you think God is calling you to do at this point in your life?

Paul's Call

My name is Paul, and I want to tell you about an incredible thing that happened to me. Oh, I should tell you that some people call me Saul. Paul or Saul, I am still the same person. I used to be very zealous in trying to stop the Jesus followers. Do you know what *zealous* means? That means I worked very hard at it. I am a devout Jew, and I believed the Jesus-followers were dangerous and needed to be stopped! I had heard there were a lot of Jesus-followers in Damascus, so I talked to the high priest and had him write letters for me to take to the synagogues in Damascus. That way I could arrest the Jesus-followers and bring them back to Jerusalem.

Now, here's where my story gets a little strange. As I was traveling to Damascus, a bright light from heaven flashed around me. I fell to the ground and heard a voice asking, "Paul, Paul, why are you harassing me?" It was Jesus speaking to me! He told me to get up and continue to Damascus, where I would be told what to do. When I got up I couldn't see. The men I was traveling with led me into Damascus, where I didn't eat or drink for three days. I spent my time praying and waiting to be told what to do.

While I was praying, God showed me that a man named Ananias would come and lay his hands on me so I could see again. And he did! Ananias was a follower of Jesus who lived in Damascus. He told me afterward that he had received a message from God to come find me. He came into the house where I was staying, laid his hands on me, and said, "Brother Saul, Jesus who appeared to you on the way to Damascus sent me so that you could see again and be filled with the Holy Spirit." Ananias also said that God told him I had been chosen to deliver God's message to other people.

When Ananias finished speaking I could see again! From that point on I began preaching about Jesus in the synagogues. Many people were confused by my sudden change of heart, but I didn't let that stop me. Jesus had appeared to me, Paul, even though I had been persecuting his followers! Jesus called me to help spread the good news of God's love, and I listened.

(Based on Acts 9)

2 Called to Go

<table>
<tr><td>

Objectives

The children will
- hear Acts 13 and 14.
- learn about Paul's first missionary journey.
- discover that God called Paul and Barnabas to travel and preach about Jesus.
- explore where God is calling them to share the good news.

</td><td>

Bible Story

Paul's First Missionary Journey: Acts 13–14

Bible Verse

We are speaking through Christ in the presence of God, as those who are sincere and as those who are sent from God. (2 Corinthians 2:17)

</td></tr>
</table>

Focus for the Teacher

God called Paul for a special purpose: to bring God's name to the "Gentiles, kings, and Israelites" (Acts 9:15). Following his encounter with Jesus on the road to Damascus, Paul essentially spent the rest of his life fulfilling the mission for which God had chosen him. The last half of the Book of Acts tells of Paul's travels.

During the remainder of this study, we will be taking a look at the journeys of Paul. These are missionary journeys. Paul traveled throughout the Holy Land, Asia Minor, and Europe proclaiming the word of God and making disciples. Paul preached the good news to Jews and Gentiles (non-Jews). Although there is a tendency to say that the Gentiles believed Paul and the Jews persecuted him, the actuality is that some but not all Gentiles converted to Christianity. In the same manner, some but not all Jews felt threatened by Paul's teaching. Many Jews converted to Christianity. Remember that Paul himself was a Jew.

On his first journey, Paul traveled with Barnabas. They were commissioned from the church in Antioch, which was in Syria. The church in Antioch was the first center of Gentile Christianity. When the Jews in Jerusalem heard what was happening, they sent Barnabas to investigate. Barnabas was happy to

> Paul shared the good news with everyone he met.

see what God was accomplishing in Antioch. Barnabas then went to Tarsus, found Paul, and brought him to Antioch. Together, Barnabas and Paul taught in Antioch until the Holy Spirit sent them out on their first missionary journey.

It is easy for us today to feel far removed from Paul's mission. Few of us are called to travel to foreign lands and spread the good news that Jesus is the Messiah. However, it is worthwhile to note that as he traveled, Paul shared the good news with everyone he met. We can follow Paul's example and share the good news with persons we meet, wherever life might take us. We may be hesitant to follow Paul's example because we fear rejection. Here, too, Paul can be an example for us, as not all who heard Paul preach became believers. Yet, Paul was not to be deterred. He continued to do what he was called to do. When people rejected them, Paul and Barnabas "shook the dust from their feet" (Acts 13:51) and sought out others who were more responsive to their teachings. As you teach your children to follow Paul's example and spread the good news, remind them not to be discouraged if some people are not receptive to the news. We are the messengers. God will see that the message is delivered.

Explore Interest Groups

Be sure that adult leaders are waiting when the first child arrives. Greet and welcome the children. Get them involved in an activity that interests them and introduces the theme for the day's activities.

Make a Sailboat

- **Say:** Last week we heard about Paul becoming a follower of Jesus. Today we will hear about a journey that Paul took. Paul began his journey on a sailboat.

- Give each child a plastic lid, a marble-sized lump of modeling clay, a chenille stem piece, and a craft foam triangle.

- Invite the children to use markers to decorate the craft foam triangle that will be the sail of their boat.

- Have the children punch two holes along one side of the craft foam triangle.

- Encourage the children to weave the pipe cleaner through the holes in the craft foam triangle.

- Have the children roll their modeling clay into a ball and stick it in the middle of the plastic lid, making sure that the flat side of the lid is down on the table.

- Encourage the children to stick the pipe cleaner with the sail on it into the ball of modeling clay to complete their boat.

- Invite the children to place their boats in the water and spend some time sailing the boats.

Spread the Good News Game

- Have the children close their eyes.

- **Say:** I am going to tap some of you on the shoulder. If I tap your shoulder, don't say anything, but remember that you have been tapped.

- While the children have their eyes closed, move among them and tap two children on the shoulder.

- Have the children open their eyes.

- **Say:** If you were tapped on the shoulder, you have heard the good news. We are going to play a game to spread the good news to everybody. When I tell you to begin, everyone will move around and shake hands with each other. If you have the good news, every time you shake someone's hand give it an extra (gentle) squeeze. If you shake hands with someone who has the good news and they squeeze your hand, then you now have the good news too.

Prepare

- ✓ On a plastic tablecoth or a designated area outside, fill several plastic tubs or a large plastic swimming pool half full with water.

- ✓ Supply plastic lids (such as from yogurt or butter containers), modeling clay, chenille stems, craft foam, scissors, one-hole paper punches, and markers.

- ✓ Cut the chenille stems in half.

- ✓ Out of the craft foam, cut triangles that are approximately three inches high. The triangles do not need to be the same size.

From that point on, every time you shake someone's hand give it an extra (gentle) squeeze. Let's see how long it takes for the good news to spread.

- Encourage the children to play the game.
- After a while, stop the game and check to see how many people have received the good news.
- **Say:** When we began the game only two people had received the good news. You have done a great job of spreading the good news.
- Start the game over, choosing different children to start spreading the good news.

Prepare

✓ Supply bananas, graham cracker squares, bear-shaped graham crackers, plates, spoons, and napkins.

✓ Use a knife to make a lengthwise cut in each banana peel. Gently push the ends of the banana to open up the peel and make the banana resemble a boat.

✓ Cut the graham cracker squares in half diagonally to make triangles.

Prepare

✓ Provide copies of **Reproducible 2a: Paul's Tour Guide**.

✓ Supply pencils.

✓ *Answer*: The Holy Spirit told Paul where to travel.

Make an Edible Boat

- Have the children wash their hands.
- **Say:** In today's Bible story we are going to hear about a journey the Apostle Paul took on a boat. Right now you are going to make a boat you can eat.
- Give each child a plate, a napkin, a spoon, a banana boat, two triangle graham cracker pieces, and a handful of bear-shaped graham crackers.
- Have the children add the graham cracker triangles to their banana boat as sails.
- Encourage the children to place the bear-shaped graham crackers in their boat to represent Paul and the others on the ship.
- Say a prayer of thanks and enjoy the snack together, encouraging the children to use spoons to scoop the banana out of the peel.

Crack the Code

- Give each child a pencil and a copy of Reproducible 2a: Paul's Tour Guide.
- Encourage children to work individually or together to decode the message.

Large Group

Bring all the children together to experience the Bible story. Use a bell to alert the children to the large-group time.

Cheer for the Good News

- Lead the children in the following cheer.

    o **Leader:** I say, "Good," you say, "News." Good!
    o All: News!
    o **Leader:** Good!
    o All: News!
    o **Leader:** You say, "Good," I say, "News."
    o All: Good!
    o **Leader:** News! Say it again!
    o All: Good!
    o **Leader:** News!

- **Ask:** What is the good news? (Jesus loves us. Jesus is alive. Jesus is God's son. Jesus shows us how to live.)

- **Say:** God called Paul to tell people the good news.

Paul's First Missionary Journey

- **Say:** Our Bible story today is about Paul, just as it was last week.

- **Ask:** What do you remember about the story we heard about Paul last week?

- Encourage the children to work together to remember and tell the story of Paul's encounter with Jesus on the way to Damascus, asking questions to prompt them as necessary.

- **Say:** Remember that all our Bible stories during this study are found in the Book of Acts.

- **Ask:** What is the longer name for the Book of Acts? (Acts of the Apostles) Where do we find the Book of Acts? (in the New Testament, following the Gospels)

- Read the Bible story from Reproducible 2b: Paul's First Missionary Journey.

- **Ask:** Who decided that Paul and Barnabas should begin traveling? (the Holy Spirit) Why were they traveling? (to spread the good news) What was the good news that Paul and Barnabas were sharing? (Jesus is the Messiah and Jesus is alive)

- **Say:** Paul and Barnabas traveled to many places on their journey. Everywhere they went, they told people about Jesus.

Prepare

✓ Provide copies of **Reproducible 2b: Paul's First Missionary Journey**.

✓ If you have invited a visitor to come and read Paul's story to the class each week as suggested in Lesson 1, have this person tell the story.

Prepare

✓ Write the Bible verse on a marker board or a piece of mural paper and place it where it can easily be seen. ("We are speaking through Christ…as those who are sent from God." 2 Corinthians 2:17)

Spreading a Bible Verse

- Show the children the Bible verse.

- **Say:** Our Bible verse for today is from a letter Paul wrote to the church he had helped start in Corinth. These are Paul's words.

- Encourage the children to read the Bible verse with you.

- **Ask:** What did God send Paul to do? (help spread the good news about Jesus)

- Choose a child in the middle of the room to begin the Bible verse.

- **Say:** (Child's name) is going to read the Bible verse. Then they will say the verse again and be joined by anyone who is sitting next to them or directly in front of them or directly behind them. We will keep repeating the verse over and over. When the person next to you or in front of you or behind you says the verse, then the next time you will join in with us.

- Begin saying the verse and continue repeating it until everyone is saying the verse together.

Called to Go

- **Say:** Paul was a missionary.

- **Ask:** What is a missionary? (someone who travels to different places to tell people about God)

- **Say:** The Holy Spirit led Paul to many different places to tell people about Jesus. Paul shared the good news with everyone he met. Not all of us are called to be missionaries like Paul. But we can tell people about Jesus wherever we go.

- **Ask:** Where are some places that you go during the week? (home, school, church, sports practice, and so on)

- **Say:** Everywhere you are, you can look for ways to share the good news with people, with your actions and your words.

- **Ask:** What are some ways you can share the good news?

- Allow children an opportunity to share their ideas.

- Dismiss children to their small groups.

Small Groups

Divide the children into small groups. You may organize the groups around age levels or around readers and nonreaders. Keep the groups small, with a maximum of ten children in each group. You may need to have more than one group of each age level.

Young Children (Ages 5-7)

- **Say:** Just like Paul, we are called by God to share the good news with others.

- **Ask:** If you were going to tell someone the good news, what would you say?

- Give the children an opportunity to share their ideas with each other.

- **Say:** Those are all great ideas of things to tell people. Today we are going to make some posters to share the good news. We will put some of the posters up in our building, and you may take some of the posters home to put up wherever you choose. Paul and Barnabas went together to share the good news, so we are going to work together in pairs to make our posters.

- Have the children find partners.

- Give each pair of children several pieces of paper, and encourage them to make posters to share the good news.

- Encourage each pair of children to make at least three posters—one to hang up and one for each child to take home.

- When the posters are finished, have the partners take at least one of their posters and hang it up somewhere in your building.

- Encourage the children to take some of their posters home and find a place to hang them where others will see them.

- **Say:** This week, remember to look for ways to share God's love with everyone you meet.

- **Pray:** God, thank you for the good news of Jesus. Help us to look for ways we can be like Paul and share the good news.

Prepare

✓ Provide paper and markers.

✓ Assist younger children with writing as needed.

Prepare

✓ Find the names and addresses of some missionaries the children can write to. If your church sponsors a missionary, that would be a good choice. Another place to look is on the state or national website for your church's denomination. You may choose one missionary for all the children to write to, or you may choose several missionaries and let the children choose whom they wish to write to.

✓ Provide paper, pens or pencils, envelopes, and a world map or atlas.

Older Children (Ages 8–11)

- **Say:** Paul was a missionary. He traveled many places to tell people about Jesus and share God's love.

- **Ask:** What do you think it would be like to be a missionary? Do you think it would be easy work? Why or why not? Do you think missionaries ever get discouraged?

- **Say:** Paul kept preaching and spreading the good news for many years. He visited churches that he had started to see how things were going. When he couldn't visit, he wrote encouraging letters. Today we are going to write letters to some missionaries. Our letters can help encourage them to keep up their good work!

- **Ask:** What kinds of things could we write that would be encouraging? (God is with you. Keep up the good work. Thanks for sharing God's love with others.)

- Let the children share their ideas with each other.

- Tell the children the names of the missionaries you have found and where they are working.

- Using the map or atlas, help the children find the places where the missionaries are at work.

- Invite each child to write a letter to a missionary.

- Have the children place the letter they have written in an envelope.

- Help the children address the envelopes.

- **Say:** On Paul's first missionary journey he traveled with his friend Barnabas. Paul did most of the preaching, and Barnabas was his helper and encourager. The letters you have written will encourage missionaries, like Barnabas encouraged Paul.

- Have the children hold the letters they have written while you pray.

- **Pray:** God, bless these letters we have written, that they may encourage those who are sharing the good news of your love with other people. Help us find ways to share the good news wherever we are. Amen.

- After class, mail the letters the children have written.

Paul's Tour Guide

The Apostle Paul went on at least four different journeys during his time as a missionary. How did Paul decide where to travel to spread the good news about Jesus? Decode the message below to discover Paul's "tour guide." (Hint: A=1, B=2, C=3, and so on.)

___ ___ ___   ___ ___ ___ ___   ___ ___ ___ ___ ___ ___
20-8-5   8-15-12-25   19-16-9-18-9-20

___ ___ ___ ___   ___ ___ ___ ___   ___ ___ ___ ___ ___
20-15-12-4   16-1-21-12   23-8-5-18-5

___ ___   ___ ___ ___ ___ ___ ___ .
20-15   20-18-1-22-5-12

Paul's First Missionary Journey

Hello, it's me again, Paul! Today I'm going to tell you about my first missionary journey. After Jesus spoke to me on the road to Damascus and I began to follow him, I spent time studying and learning more about Jesus. Then I spent a year teaching and preaching at the church in Antioch with my friend Barnabas. Then one day the Holy Spirit let us know that Barnabas and I were to be sent out to spread the good news elsewhere. Our friends at the church in Antioch prayed for us and sent us on our way.

Barnabas and I traveled many places on our journey. Often we traveled by boat, though sometimes we traveled on foot to cities farther inland. We went to Seleucia, Salamis, Paphos, Perga, Pisidia, Iconium, Lystra, Derbe, and Attalia. I told you we went to a lot of places!

Everywhere we went, we preached God's word in the synagogue. When we went to the synagogue, we listened to the reading of the Law and the prophets. Often, the officials of the synagogue would invite us to speak. Then I would stand up and begin to preach. I always began by reminding them of our history—of God's faithfulness to our ancestors. Then I would share the good news with everyone there. I told them about Jesus and how he had been raised from the dead. I told them Jesus was the Savior whom God had promised to send. After the meeting, many people, both Jews and Gentiles, spoke to Barnabas and me. We encouraged them to remain faithful to God. A great number of Jews and Gentiles came to believe that Jesus is the Messiah. It was very exciting! We helped start churches in some of the places we visited.

Sometimes our travels were difficult. The crowds that gathered to hear us preach made some of the synagogue leaders nervous. A few times, some of the people became angry with us and made us leave town. Then we would travel to the next place where the Holy Spirit sent us.

When we finally headed for home, we stopped in some of the places we had visited previously. It was great to see the work being done by the churches that we had helped to start. When we returned to Antioch, we told the church there about our journey and all the things God had done through us.

(Based on Acts 13–14)

3 Called to Be Faithful

<table>
<tr><td>

Objectives

The children will
- hear Acts 16.
- learn about Paul and Silas being thrown in prison.
- discover that Paul continued to spread the good news even in difficult circumstances.
- explore ways that they can remain faithful to God.

</td><td>

Bible Story

Paul Goes to Prison: Acts 16

Bible Verse

I can endure all these things through the power of the one who gives me strength. (Philippians 4:13)

</td></tr>
</table>

Focus for the Teacher

Once again this week, we are journeying with Paul as he continued to share the good news with everyone he met. This week's Bible story is from Paul's second missionary journey.

Everywhere Paul went he searched for opportunities to preach and share the good news. Paul's news wasn't always welcome, however. Paul was put in prison several times. Some of his letters were written from prison.

During his second missionary journey, Paul and his traveling partner, Silas, were thrown into prison for healing a slave woman. Though healing a slave woman sounds like a good thing to do, especially for the woman concerned, the woman's owners were not pleased. Once the slave woman was healed, they would no longer be able to use the woman as a fortune-teller to make money for them. The owners of the slave woman had Paul and Silas thrown into prison.

The experience of Paul and Silas in prison illustrates Paul's zealousness in spreading the good news. While Paul and Silas were in prison, there was an earthquake that opened the prison

> ## In a difficult situation, Paul saw an opportunity.

doors and broke their chains. Presented with an opportunity to escape, Paul and Silas instead stayed and witnessed to the jailer. In a difficult situation, Paul saw an opportunity.

Through Paul's travels and his efforts to share the good news with everyone he met, the word of God spread and the early church continued to grow. Had Paul stayed at home, you might not be preparing this lesson, because it is difficult to believe in something you don't know about!

It might be tempting to applaud Paul's efforts and then sit back and assume that the work of spreading the good news is done. However, there are still people today who need to hear this good news—the news that Jesus is alive. Fellowship with others and intensive instruction were central to Paul's ministry. When we gather together as a community of faith for worship and Sunday school, we are recognizing what Paul knew: that for the church to grow and thrive, people need to meet together and learn about God. When we invite others to join us at church, we are helping to spread the good news, just as Paul did.

Explore Interest Groups

Be sure that adult leaders are waiting when the first child arrives. Greet and welcome the children. Get them involved in an activity that interests them and introduces the theme for the day's activities.

Walk Through a Piece of Paper

- Hold up a sheet of paper.
- **Ask:** Do you think I can walk through this piece of paper? Do you think our entire class would fit through this piece of paper?
- Give each child a piece of paper and a pair of scissors.
- Have the children fold their paper in half, bringing the long sides together.
- Show the children how to cut the paper in the following way:
  - o Begin cutting on the folded edge near one end of the paper, and cut through almost to the other side.
  - o Cut a line parallel to the first cut but beginning at the nonfolded edge of the paper, again stopping before they reach the edge.
  - o Continue cutting parallel lines, alternating starting the cuts on the folded and nonfolded edges of the paper. The last cut should begin on the folded edge.
- Have the children lay their paper flat on the table, still folded.
- **Say:** Right now your paper looks like jail bars. Today we are going to learn about a time Paul was in jail.
- On the folded edge of the paper, have the children cut along the fold on every strip except the first and last strip.
- Have the children open up the paper that will now be a large circle that can easily be walked through.
- Challenge the children in your class to see if they can cut a piece of paper that your entire class can fit in. The closer together the cuts are made, the larger the circle will be.
- Lay the resulting circle on the floor and see if everyone can stand inside the paper circle.

Graham Cracker Earthquakes

- Have the children wash their hands.
- **Ask:** Do you know what an earthquake is? Have you ever experienced an earthquake?
- **Say:** We are going to hear about an earthquake in our Bible story today. Right now we are going to learn more about how earthquakes happen.
- Give each child a square of waxed paper.

Prepare

- ✓ Supply paper and scissors.
- ✓ *Tip*: For young children, draw lines on the paper as a cutting guide.

Prepare

- ✓ Supply graham crackers, miniature marshmallows, frosting, plastic spoons, waxed paper, napkins, and wet wipes.

Called to Be Faithful

- Give each child a spoonful of frosting. Show the children a graham cracker. Encourage the children to spread their frosting onto the waxed paper, in a thick layer slightly larger than the graham cracker.
- Give each child a graham cracker.
- Have each child break the graham cracker into two squares along the perforation.
- Have each child lay the two graham cracker squares on top of the frosting layer, with the broken edges of the graham cracker together.
- **Say:** The frosting on your waxed paper represents magma. Magma is a semiliquid substance underneath the earth's surface. The graham crackers represent the earth's surface. The surface of the earth is not one large piece, but instead is made up of large pieces or "plates."
- Give each child about eight marshmallows.
- Encourage the children to build marshmallow towers on top of their graham crackers.
- **Say:** Sometimes temperature changes or other events below the earth's surface will cause pieces of the earth to shift and rub against one another.
- Have the children slide one graham cracker square toward them while sliding the other graham cracker square away, observing the crumbs that form as the graham crackers rub against one another.
- **Ask:** What happened to your marshmallow towers?
- Let the children eat their earthquake experiments.

While in Prison

- Give each child a pencil and a copy of Reproducible 3a: While in Prison.
- Encourage children to work individually or together to solve the puzzle.
- Have children look up Acts 16:25 to check their answers.

Prepare

✓ Provide copies of **Reproducible 3a: While in Prison.**

✓ Supply pencils and Bibles.

✓ *Answer*: They prayed and sang hymns to God.

Large Group

Bring all the children together to experience the Bible story. Use a bell to alert the children to the large-group time.

Paul's Second Missionary Journey Begins

- **Say:** Today we are continuing to learn about the Apostle Paul. Last week we heard about Paul's first missionary journey. Today's story is about something that happened during Paul's second missionary journey.
- Read the story from Reproducible 3b: Paul Goes to Prison. When you get to the part about Paul being put in prison, step behind the crepe paper streamers and tell the story from behind them until the end of the story when Paul and Silas are freed.
- **Ask:** Why were Paul and Silas put in prison? (for healing the slave woman) Why were the owners of the slave woman upset with Paul and Silas? (because the woman would no longer make money for them) How did Paul and Silas spend their time in prison? (singing and praying) Why do you think Paul and Silas stayed after the earthquake opened the doors and broke their chains? (We don't really know. Maybe they sensed they would have a chance to witness to the jailer.)
- **Say:** Wherever Paul went, he shared God's love and told people about Jesus. He even told people about Jesus when he was in prison! Paul was faithful to God even during difficult times. We can follow Paul's example and always be faithful to God.

Bible Verse Beat

- Show the children the Bible verse.
- Invite the children to read the Bible verse with you.
- **Say:** Remember that our Bible verses are from letters Paul wrote. This verse is from a letter Paul wrote to the church in Philippi. Paul wrote this letter while he was in prison.
- **Ask:** Who is speaking in this verse? (Paul) What does the word *endure* mean? (to deal with or put up with) What is Paul enduring? (being in prison) Who is Paul referring to as the "one who gives me strength"? (God)
- **Say:** We are going to read our Bible verse again, but this time we are going to say it to a steady beat.
- Invite the children to clap along with you as you clap a steady beat. Once the beat is established, have the children read the verse with you, saying one syllable per clap. It may take a couple of tries to get it just right.
- Try saying the verse to a foot stomping beat.
- For an added challenge, have half the children clap the beat and half the children stomp the beat while everyone reads the verse.

Prepare

- ✓ Provide copies of **Reproducible 3b: Paul Goes to Prison.**
- ✓ In one part of your story-telling area, attach black crepe paper streamers from the ceiling using tape or pushpins. Space the streamers to resemble prison bars. Let the streamers hang down to the floor.
- ✓ If you have invited a visitor to come and read Paul's story to the class each week as suggested in Lesson 1, have this person tell the story.

Prepare

- ✓ Write the Bible verse on a marker board or a piece of mural paper and place it where it can easily be seen. ("I can endure all these things through the power of the one who gives me strength." Philippians 4:13)

Prepare

✓ If you are not familiar with the song "Hallelu, Hallelu," you can print free music and listen to the melody online.

✓ The lyrics are:

> Hallelu, hallelu,
>   hallelu, hallelujah
> Praise ye the Lord.
> Hallelu, hallelu,
>   hallelu, hallelujah
> Praise ye the Lord.
> Praise ye the Lord.
> Hallelujah.
> Praise ye the Lord.
> Hallelujah.
> Praise ye the Lord.
> Hallelujah.
> Praise ye the Lord!

Praise God with Singing

- **Say:** In our Bible story today, Paul goes to prison. He spends the time in prison praying and singing. Let's praise God by singing.

- Teach the children the song "Hallelu, Hallelu."

- Divide the children into two groups.

- Have one group sing the "Hallelujahs" and the other group sing the "Praise ye the Lord."

- Have the children stand up when it is their turn to sing and sit down when they are not singing.

- Sing the song several times, getting faster each time.

Called to Be Faithful

- **Say:** Paul was faithful to God even when he was in difficult situations. He continued to spread the good news even when he was in prison. Paul and Silas knew God was with them no matter where they were. Singing and praying helped them remember God's faithfulness. We just sang. Now we are going to pray. I am going to have you close your eyes while I say our prayer. At various times during the prayer I will invite you to take a deep breath and then let it out.

- Invite the children to find a comfortable sitting position and close their eyes.

- Read the following statements slowly and calmly:
    - o God, we thank you for being with us when we arc happy, joyful, or excited.
    - o Take a deep breath . . . and let it out.
    - o God, we thank you for being with us when we are sad, hurt, or afraid.
    - o Take a deep breath . . . and let it out.
    - o Thank you, God, for your never-ending love for us, and for your constant presence with us.
    - o Take a deep breath . . . and let it out.
    - o Help us to remain faithful to you at all times, God, when life is easy and when life is difficult.
    - o Take a deep breath . . . and let it out.
    - o Amen.

- Invite the children to open their eyes.

- Dismiss children to their small groups.

Small Groups

Divide the children into small groups. You may organize the groups around age levels or around readers and nonreaders. Keep the groups small, with a maximum of ten children in each group. You may need to have more than one group of each age level.

Young Children (Ages 5-7)

- **Say:** Let's review today's story.

- Invite the children to share what they remember about the story, asking questions to prompt them as needed.

- **Ask:** How do you think Paul and Silas felt when they were thrown in prison? (scared, angry, nervous) Have you ever felt that way?

- **Say:** It would have been easy for Paul and Silas to feel that God had abandoned them when they were thrown into prison, but instead they remembered that God was always with them, no matter what.

- **Ask:** Is it more difficult to remember God is with you when you are sad or afraid? What helps you remember that God is always with you? What did Paul and Silas do to help them feel God's presence while they were in prison? (prayed and sang hymns)

- Give each child a piece of white paper and a white crayon.

- **Say:** You are going to make a picture that will help you remember to pray whether you are feeling happy, sad, excited, or scared.

- Invite each child to use the white crayon to write the word PRAY in large letters on the piece of paper.

- **Ask:** Do you think this picture will help you remember to pray? Why or why not?

- Show the children how to use the side of the marker tip to color back and forth over the paper to make the writing appear.

- **Say:** Now it is easier to see the prayer reminder. When you take it home, put your reminder someplace where you will see it often.

- **Pray:** God, thank you for stories of Paul that remind us you are always with us, in good times and bad times. Help us feel your presence and share that love with everyone we meet. Amen.

Prepare

✓ Supply white paper, white crayons, and markers.

Prepare

✓ Provide index cards and pencils.

Older Children (Ages 8-11)

- **Say:** Today we heard about Paul and Silas being thrown in prison.

- **Ask:** Do you think Paul and Silas wanted to be in prison?

- **Say:** Life doesn't always go smoothly. Sometimes we encounter challenges and life is difficult. But we know that God is always with us, no matter what.

- **Ask:** When is it easy for you to feel God's presence with you? When is it more difficult for you to feel God's presence?

- **Say:** While Paul and Silas were in prison, they sang hymns and prayed. Singing and praying probably helped them remember that God was with them. There are many ways to pray. Today we are each going to write a sentence prayer. Sentence prayers are short prayers that can be repeated often and are useful if you don't know what to pray.

- Give each child an index card and a pencil.

- **Ask:** What are some names we use for God?

- Encourage children to come up with as many different names for God as they can.

- **Say:** Choose your favorite name for God and write it on your card.

- Give children time to write.

- **Say:** Now think about something you might want to ask God for when life gets challenging. Maybe "Help me make it through this day" or "Show me what you want me to do" or "Help me feel you near me." Write the sentence on your card.

- Give children time to write.

- **Say:** You have made your own sentence prayer. Sometimes it is helpful to pray your sentence prayer in rhythm with your breathing. For example, if your prayer is "Loving God, guide me on your path," you might pray, "Loving God," while breathing in and "guide me on your path" while breathing out. This is a simple way to help you focus on your prayer.

- Give the children some time to pray their prayers individually in silence.

- **Say:** Amen.

While in Prison

On Paul's second missionary journey, his friend Silas went with him. Paul and Silas traveled, and everywhere they went they told people about Jesus. One time Paul and Silas were arrested and thrown in prison. What did Paul and Silas do while they were in prison? To find out, write the letter that appears twice in each word below on the line. When you are finished, read down to discover what Paul and Silas did while they were in prison. Look up Acts 16:25 to check your answer.

little	_____	Silas	_____
hush	_____	Adam	_____
Eve	_____	runny	_____
anybody	_____	egg	_____
apple	_____	rhythm	_____
carrot	_____	heyday	_____
sailboat	_____	mime	_____
dryly	_____	sunny	_____
energy	_____	Jesus	_____
middle	_____		
		title	_____
canal	_____	octopus	_____
none	_____		
dandy	_____	gauge	_____
		good	_____
		riddle	_____

Paul Goes to Prison

Hi, it's Paul again. Today I want to tell you about a time my friend Silas and I were preaching in Philippi. This happened during my second missionary journey. We were in Philippi staying with our friend Lydia. Every day we would go to the place of prayer down by the river to preach and teach people about Jesus.

One day as we were going to the place of prayer, we met a slave woman who had a spirit that enabled her to predict the future. Her owners used her to make money by having her tell fortunes for other people. This woman began following us and shouting, "These people are servants of the Most High God! They are proclaiming a way of salvation for you!"

For several days this woman followed us and shouted as we walked to the place of prayer. Finally I turned around and said to the spirit in the woman, "In the name of Jesus Christ, I command you to leave her!" The spirit left the slave woman immediately.

Now, you would think this was a good thing, but the owners of the slave woman were not happy with me. You see, by healing the woman of her spirit, I had taken away their way of using her to make money. They grabbed Silas and me and dragged us before the authorities. The authorities gave orders to have us beaten and thrown in prison.

So there Silas and I were in prison. Now, it would have been easy to get discouraged at this point. But we knew God was with us. We sang hymns and prayed to God all through the night.

Around midnight there was a violent earthquake that shook the prison. The doors flew open and everyone's chains came loose. When the jailer woke up and saw the open doors of the prison, he thought we had all escaped. Knowing he would get in trouble for the escape, he became very upset.

We shouted out to him, "Don't worry! We're still here!"

The jailer came and saw that Silas and I had stayed. We took that opportunity to tell him about Jesus. We preached to him and everyone else in his house. That night the jailer and his entire household were baptized.

The next morning Silas and I were released from prison. Being in prison is no fun. But even in prison we were able to do God's work.

(Based on Acts 16)

4 Called to Love

<table>
<tr><td>

Objectives

The children will
- hear Acts 18 and 1 Corinthians 13.
- learn about Paul starting the church at Corinth.
- discover that Paul encouraged Christians to love each other.
- explore what loving one another means in their own lives.

</td><td>

Bible Story

Paul Visits Corinth: Acts 18 and 1 Corinthians 13

Bible Verse

Now faith, hope, and love remain—these three things—and the greatest of these is love.
(1 Corinthians 13:13)

</td></tr>
</table>

Focus for the Teacher

On Paul's journeys to spread the good news, he often began by teaching in the local Jewish synagogue. This was a place that he could spread the news of Jesus to the Jews who were expecting a Messiah. As the believers began to establish their own practices, it became necessary to gather in a place other than the synagogue. Many of the first churches they formed met in the homes of believers. The early church met to share a meal and to worship together by praying, singing, and teaching. Because of the importance of the household in the formation of the church, the church is sometimes described as the "household of God."

> The love that flows from God through us is infinite.

During Paul's second missionary journey he visited Corinth. Paul stayed in Corinth for eighteen months, becoming friends with the Jesus followers there. While in Corinth, Paul stayed with a couple named Priscilla and Aquila, who were tentmakers. Paul had learned tentmaking as a trade, and it was likely that this common interest brought them together initially. Priscilla and Aquila worked with Paul to spread the good news. Their house served as one of the meeting places of the early church.

As Paul continued his missionary journey, he heard that the believers in Corinth were struggling and arguing among themselves. Paul wrote to his friends in the Corinthian church to encourage and advise them. Integral to Paul's advice were his thoughts on love, presented in 1 Corinthians 13. Love, Paul ably put forth, should be at the center of the community's thoughts and actions. Love is an essential element of a believer's life.

Paul's chapter on love is often read at wedding ceremonies. While this is certainly appropriate—Paul's description applies to any circumstance in which love is found—romantic love was not what Paul had in mind when he wrote these words. The love that Paul describes begins with God. God's love claims us and, through us, reaches out to others. We, who have been loved by God, honor that love by sharing it with others.

The love that flows from God through us is infinite. It never ends. The things of this life come and go, but love endures. If we were to take seriously that our loving was our enduring legacy, how would we approach life differently? How would that concept shape our relationships and our actions?

Explore Interest Groups

Be sure that adult leaders are waiting when the first child arrives. Greet and welcome the children. Get them involved in an activity that interests them and introduces the theme for the day's activities.

Sew a Tent

- **Say:** We have been learning about the Apostle Paul. Before he became a follower of Jesus, Paul had learned to be a tentmaker. During Paul's second missionary journey he stayed with a couple who also made tents. Their names were Priscilla and Aquila. Today you will make a tent.
- Give each child two index cards.
- **Say:** In the days of Paul, Priscilla, and Aquila, tents were made by sewing pieces of leather or fabric together. The pieces of leather were punctured and then sewn together.
- Encourage each child to place the two index cards on top of each other and use the paper punch to punch holes along one of the long sides.
- Have each child cut a piece of yarn about twelve inches long.
- Have each child thread the yarn through the holes on one end of the index cards and tie a knot to secure the yarn.
- Encourage each child to use the yarn to sew the cards together.
- Have each child secure the end of the yarn by tying a knot.
- Invite each child to pull the open edges of the index cards apart and stand up the tent.
- Encourage the children to decorate their tent with markers.

Prepare

✓ Provide index cards, yarn, scissors, paper punches, and markers.

✓ *Tip:* To provide a challenge for older children, encourage them to make a bigger tent by sewing several cards together.

Infinity Relay

- **Ask:** Do you know what infinity is?
- **Say:** Infinity is a term that is used for something that is never-ending. The infinity symbol looks like a number 8 lying on its side. For this race, you will walk a path that looks like an infinity symbol around the two chairs.
- Divide the children into two teams and assign each team to one of the race areas.
- **Say:** When I tell you to start, have each person in your team take a turn doing the infinity walk. You may walk quickly, but do not run. When each member of your team has completed the infinity walk, sit down so I will know you have finished.

Prepare

✓ Set up two identical race areas. For each race area, place two chairs approximately four feet apart. Make sure there is room for the children to walk around the chairs on all sides.

- Have the children do the infinity relay.

- For an extra challenge, have the children do the infinity relay using the following actions: skipping, hopping on one foot, and walking backward.

- **Say:** Today we are talking about love. God's love for us is infinite—it never ends.

Prepare

✓ Cut a large sheet of mural paper. At the top of the paper write the words "Love is . . ." Place the paper where the children can see it.

What Is Love?

- **Ask:** How would you describe love? How would you complete the statement, "Love is . . . "?

- Give the children an opportunity to complete the statement, "Love is . . . "

- Write the children's statements on the mural paper.

- Save the statements on the mural paper to be used later in the lesson.

Prepare

✓ Provide copies of **Reproducible 4a: The Greatest Thing**.

✓ Supply pencils.

✓ *Answers*: PAIL, FAIL, FALL, BALL, BALE, BAKE, BIKE, LIKE, LIVE, LOVE

The Greatest Thing

- Give each child a pencil and a copy of Reproducible 4a: The Greatest Thing.

- Encourage children to work individually or together to solve the puzzle.

The Call: Children's Leader Guide

Large Group

Bring all the children together to experience the Bible story. Use a bell to alert the children to the large-group time.

Loving Words

- **Say:** Today we are going to hear how Paul described what love is. I am guessing that you already have a good idea of what it means to act lovingly. I am going to read you some words. If the words I read are loving words, shout out, "That's love!" If the words I read are not loving, say, "No, no, no!"

- Read the following statements and encourage the children to respond appropriately.

    o Take your time. I'm not in a hurry. (That's love!)
    o Hurry up! Can't you see that I have things to do! (No, no, no!)
    o I like the picture you drew. Tell me about it. (That's love!)
    o Get out of my way! (No, no, no!)
    o That is a cool bike! I bet it can go really fast. (That's love!)
    o Why don't I have new tennis shoes like he does? (No, no, no!)
    o I'll bet I did better on that test than you did. (No, no, no!)
    o Good try! (That's love!)
    o What did you do that for? I knew it wouldn't work. (No, no, no!)
    o It looks like that was hard to do. (That's love!)
    o Give me some cake! (No, no, no!)
    o Thank you for helping me. (That's love!)

- **Say:** Great job! You know about love—I can tell.

Paul Visits Corinth

- **Say:** Last week we heard about Paul being thrown in prison during his second missionary journey. This week's story is also about Paul's second missionary journey.

- Read the story from Reproducible 4b: Paul Visits Corinth.

- **Ask:** Where did Paul stay while he was in Corinth? (with Aquila and Priscilla) Where did the church in Corinth meet? (in homes) What do you think it would be like to have our church meet at your house?

- **Say:** Paul stayed in Corinth for a long time, a year and a half. During that time he became good friends with the people there. That's why it made him sad when he heard they were arguing with each other after he left.

- **Ask:** What did Paul do when he heard the believers in Corinth weren't getting along? (He wrote them a letter.) What did Paul remind them of in his letter? (They were supposed to love each other.)

Prepare

✓ Provide copies of **Reproducible 4b: Paul Visits Corinth**.

✓ If you have invited a visitor to come and read Paul's story to the class each week as suggested in Lesson 1, have this person tell the story.

Called to Love

- **Say:** Sometimes we get so busy trying to do the right thing that we forget the most important thing—love. God loves us and we are to share that love with everyone we meet.

Prepare

✓ Write the Bible verse on a marker board or a piece of mural paper, and place it where it can easily be seen. ("Now faith, hope, and love remain—these three things—and the greatest of these is love." 1 Corinthians 13:13)

Bible Verse in Three Parts

- **Say:** Our Bible verse today is from one of the letters Paul wrote to the believers in Corinth.

- Encourage the children to read the Bible verse with you.

- **Say:** Now we are going to divide our verse into three parts. The first part will be "Now faith, hope, and love remain." The second part will be "these three things." And the third part will be "and the greatest of these is love."

- Divide the children into three groups.

- **Say:** The first group that I point to will say the first part of the verse, the second group that I point to will say the second part of the verse, and the third group that I point to will say the last part of the verse.

- Lead the children in saying the Bible verse three times, having a different group begin the verse each time.

Prepare

✓ Hang the "Love is . . ." statements completed earlier where they can be seen.

Called to Love

- **Say:** We have heard Paul's description of love. Earlier, some of you described what love is. We are going to use your statements about love as a litany. I will read the "Love is . . ." statements. After each statement we will all respond by saying, "Love is the greatest!"

- Read the "Love is . . ." statements the children came up with, pausing after each statement for the response.

- **Pray:** God, thank you for loving us! Help us remember to show love in all our actions. Amen.

- Dismiss the children to their small groups.

Small Groups

Divide the children into small groups. You may organize the groups around age levels or around readers and nonreaders. Keep the groups small, with a maximum of ten children in each group. You may need to have more than one group of each age level.

Young Children (Ages 5-7)

- **Say:** While Paul was traveling on his missionary journeys, he told people about the life and teachings of Jesus.

- **Ask:** What did Jesus teach about love? (God loves us. We are to love each other. Love your enemies.)

- **Say:** God loves us, and we pass that love on to other people.

- **Ask:** Do you like to get mail? How does it make you feel when you get something in the mail?

- **Say:** At the time that Paul wrote his letter to the Corinthians, people didn't get mail very often. Letters had to be hand-delivered by messenger. The people at the church in Corinth were probably excited to get Paul's letter. Today we are going to make thinking-of-you cards. These cards will be delivered to people in our congregation or maybe to some who aren't in our congregation who could use a reminder that we're thinking about them.

- Tell the children who will be delivering the cards they make.

- Give all the children a piece of cardstock and have them fold it in half to form a card.

- Have the children decorate their cards.

- Encourage the children to draw pictures and write words that are cheerful.

- Remind the children to sign their first names to the cards.

- **Say:** These cards will help someone know that God loves them. This week, remember to share God's love with everyone you meet.

- **Pray:** Loving God, we thank you for your love that is patient and kind and lasts forever. Help us to love each other as you have loved us. Amen.

Prepare

- ✓ Cut cardstock in half to form two 5 ½-inch by 8½-inch pieces.

- ✓ Arrange with your pastor or another person to distribute the cards that the children make to shut-ins, to people in the hospital, or to anyone who needs a happy thought.

- ✓ Provide markers and crayons.

Prepare

✓ Supply Bibles, paper, and pencils.

Older Children (Ages 8–11)

- **Say:** Today we heard about Paul's visit to Corinth.

- **Ask:** What do you remember about today's story?

- Encourage the children to work together to retell today's story. Ask questions to prompt them as necessary.

- **Say:** When Paul wrote to the Corinthians encouraging them to treat each other with love, he was reminding them of Jesus' teachings.

- **Ask:** What did Jesus teach about love? (God loves us. We are to love each other. Love your enemies.)

- **Say:** God loves us, and we pass that love on to other people. Let's take another look at the words Paul wrote to the Corinthians about love.

- Have the children look up 1 Corinthians 13:4-8a.

- Invite the children to take turns reading the verses aloud.

- **Ask:** As you look at Paul's description of love, can you think of a time when someone has shown this kind of love to you? When has someone been kind to you or not been jealous of your accomplishments?

- Allow children an opportunity to share their experiences.

- **Say:** The type of love that Paul describes is the love we try to show to other people. It isn't always easy, and sometimes we make mistakes. Then we try again. Today we are going to personalize these verses. This is a good way to remind ourselves of the way we are to love.

- Give each child a piece of paper and a pencil.

- Have children copy 1 Corinthians 13:4-8a from the Bible, substituting their names for the words "love" and "it" each time they appear.

- Allow the children time to write.

- **Say:** Remember the descriptions of love that we talked about today, and remember to show love to everyone you meet this week.

- **Pray:** Loving God, we thank you for your love that is patient and kind and lasts forever. Help us to love each other as you have loved us. Amen.

The Greatest Thing

Beginning with the word *Paul*, change one letter at a time to form a new word using the clues below.

P A U L

Bucket ___ ___ ___ ___

To be unsuccessful in an attempt ___ ___ ___ ___

Season following summer ___ ___ ___ ___

Spherical object used to play catch ___ ___ ___ ___

Tightly compressed bundle of hay ___ ___ ___ ___

To prepare food in an oven ___ ___ ___ ___

Two-wheeled vehicle ___ ___ ___ ___

To enjoy ___ ___ ___ ___

To be alive ___ ___ ___ ___

The greatest thing, according to Paul ___ ___ ___ ___

Paul Visits Corinth

Hi, it's Paul. Today I want to tell you about my visit to the town of Corinth. I visited Corinth for the first time during my second missionary journey. When I arrived in Corinth, I met a Jew named Aquila. He and his wife, Priscilla, were tentmakers like I was. Aquila and Priscilla let me stay with them.

I began preaching in the synagogue as I usually did. Some of the Jews became upset with me—they didn't yet believe that Jesus was the Messiah. After that, I preached in the houses of Jesus followers. Quite a few people came to believe in the good news and were baptized. I stayed in Corinth for a year and a half, preaching and helping start a church. Then it was time for me to move on.

As I was traveling, I received word that the members of the church in Corinth had begun to fight among themselves. This made me sad because I knew my friends were forgetting what I had taught them about Jesus' teaching to love each other. I wasn't able to return to Corinth right away, so I wrote the Corinthians a couple of letters, reminding them of what was important and how they were to treat each other.

Here's what I wrote in one of my letters: Love is patient, love is kind, it isn't jealous, it doesn't brag, it isn't arrogant, it isn't rude, it doesn't seek its own advantage, it isn't irritable, it doesn't keep a record of complaints, it isn't happy with injustice, but it is happy with the truth. Love puts up with all things, trusts in all things, hopes for all things, endures all things. Love never fails.

I wanted to remind my friends in Corinth of the love Jesus told his followers to have for each other and the unconditional love God has for us. Everything we do should be because of love.

(Based on Acts 18 and 1 Corinthians 13)

5 Called to Give

Objectives

The children will
- hear Acts 19.
- learn about Paul's third missionary journey and the offering for Jerusalem.
- discover that the early believers supported each other in ministry.
- explore how we are called to give to God's ministry.

Bible Story

Paul's Third Missionary Journey: Acts 19

Bible Verse

God loves a cheerful giver. (2 Corinthians 9:7)

Focus for the Teacher

This week, we continue traveling with Paul by looking at his third missionary journey. It is estimated that this journey lasted over three years. Though Paul visited many places during this missionary trip, most of that time was spent in Ephesus. Paul spent over two years there teaching, preaching, and establishing churches.

Having already studied two of Paul's journeys, it is tempting to look at the Scripture for this lesson as simply another one of Paul's missionary trips and to wonder what could possibly be here that we haven't heard already. Perhaps the learning to be gained is that Paul persisted in traveling and spreading the good news. We know he encountered hardships and resistance. We can imagine there must have been days when Paul was tired, physically and spiritually. But he continued on, teaching and preaching the good news. The strength Paul needed to persevere came from God.

In each of Paul's journeys, there was an emphasis on teaching and preaching. Everywhere he went, Paul met with others and shared the good news. Fellowship and intensive instruction were central to Paul's ministry of encouragement. During Paul's

> We are part of a large community of believers.

third journey, he also encouraged each church he visited to contribute to an offering for Jerusalem.

Paul's home church in Antioch had established the offering for Jerusalem. In Acts 11, we read of some prophets from Jerusalem visiting the Antioch church. One of them predicted a severe famine in the Roman world. The famine would affect the believers in Jerusalem, and they would be in need of food. Because the Antioch church was part of the larger community of believers, they acted to take care of their brothers and sisters in Jerusalem. It did not matter that the famine would not affect them; they recognized the need of others and addressed it by taking an offering for Jerusalem.

During his third journey, Paul invited the churches he visited to contribute to this offering for Jerusalem. The offering would help the believers in Jerusalem but would also build relationships among the churches. The early churches were not individual pockets of believers who developed their own theology. Instead, each church was part of a large community of believers. Likewise, though we worship in our own church, we are a part of a large community of believers. We are all connected through Jesus and are called to support one another.

Explore Interest Groups

Be sure that adult leaders are waiting when the first child arrives. Greet and welcome the children. Get them involved in an activity that interests them and introduces the theme for the day's activities.

Collaborative Art Project

- **Say:** To collaborate means to work together. Today we are going to collaborate on an art project. Each one of you will make a piece of the project, and then we will put them together to make something even better.

- Give each child a cardstock square.

- **Say:** Each of you may decorate your square however you'd like. Somewhere in your design, include a cross. Try to decorate the entire surface of your square.

- Invite children to draw designs on their squares.

- When the children have finished their squares, encourage them to lay the squares face down and touching each other, to form a large square or rectangle.

- With the decorated sides face down, tape all the children's squares together.

- Carefully turn the art project over.

- **Say:** Each one of you created a small square, but when we put them together we made something bigger. As followers of Jesus, we are called to collaborate in doing God's work.

- Hang the collaborative project in your classroom.

Prepare
- ✓ Cut cardstock into four-inch squares.
- ✓ Provide markers and tape.

Distribute Equally

- Divide the class into groups of eight to ten children each.

- Give each child a bowl.

- Show the children the container of beads.

- **Say:** As I bring around the container of beads, I want each of you to grab a handful of beads and place them in your bowl.

- Invite each child to grab a handful of beads.

- **Say:** Now work together in your group to make sure all of you have an equal number of beads in your bowls.

- Encourage the children to redistribute the beads equally.

- Place all the beads back in the large container, have the children form different groups, and repeat the activity two more times.

- **Ask:** Did any group start out with every person having the same number of beads? What process did you use to make things equal?

Prepare
- ✓ Provide plastic beads and bowls.
- ✓ Place all the beads in a large container. If you have a large class, have several large containers of beads for faster distribution.

- **Say:** If you had extra beads, you were able to help those who had fewer beads.
- **Ask:** Did anyone need to share beads one time we did the activity and receive beads another time?
- **Say:** When we have abundance, we share with others. Sometimes we are the ones sharing, and sometimes we are the ones receiving.
- Collect all the beads.

Knowing the True God

- **Say:** As Paul traveled, he preached that there is only one God. Paul taught people about God's love and about how God wanted them to live. I am going to read some statements. If the statement describes a way you think God wants you to live, do five jumping jacks. If the statement does not describe a way God wants you to live, stand very still.
- Have the children stand up and spread out.
- Read the following statements and encourage the children to respond.
    - o I can show love to my family. (Jumping jacks)
    - o I can be friends only with people who believe in God. (Stand still)
    - o I can tell other people about Jesus. (Jumping jacks)
    - o I can invite someone to attend church and Sunday school with me. (Jumping jacks)
    - o I can skip church whenever I get a better offer or when I just don't feel like going. (Stand still)
    - o I can treat everyone with respect, even when we disagree. (Jumping jacks)
    - o If I go to church on Sunday, then I can forget about God the rest of the week. (Stand still)
    - o When I am with kids who don't go to church, I can pretend I don't believe in God. (Stand still)
    - o I can share what I have so I can help someone in need. (Jumping jacks)
- Invite children to come up with additional statements describing ways God wants them to live or ways God does not want them to live, and share these statements with the class.

Prepare

✓ Provide copies of **Reproducible 5a: Giving for God**.

✓ Supply pencils and Bibles.

Giving for God

- Give each child a pencil and a copy of Reproducible 5a: Giving for God.
- Encourage children to work individually or together to solve the puzzle.
- Have children look up 2 Corinthians 9:7 to check their answers.

Large Group

Bring all the children together to experience the Bible story. Use a bell to alert the children to the large-group time.

Rearrange, Still the Same

- **Ask:** How many children are in our class today?
- Have the children count off to determine how many children are present.
- Divide the children into four groups, having the groups stand in different areas of the room. It is not necessary to have equal numbers in each group.
- **Ask:** Now how many children are in our class today? (the same number)
- Now divide the children into six groups, having the groups stand in different areas of the room.
- **Ask:** Now how many children are in our class today? (the same number)
- **Say:** It doesn't matter where you are standing in the room; you are still a part of our class. We are one class no matter how many groups we split into. In today's Bible story, Paul reminds people that all of Jesus' followers are one family, no matter where they worship.

Paul's Third Missionary Journey

- Give each child a pencil and a copy of Reproducible 5b: Paul's Third Missionary Journey.
- **Ask:** What person do you think our Bible story is about today? (Paul) Which book of the Bible tells about Paul's missionary journeys? (Acts) Where do we find Acts in the Bible? (in the New Testament, following the gospels)
- Have the children find Acts in their Bibles.
- **Say:** We have learned that Paul did a lot of traveling. Today we are going to read about the third journey he took.
- **Ask:** Why was Paul traveling? (to share the good news) What is the good news? (Jesus is alive. Jesus loves you.)
- **Say:** As Paul traveled, he reminded believers to give to the offering for Jerusalem.
- **Ask:** Why was this offering being taken? (to help Jesus' followers in Jerusalem)
- **Say:** Most of the people Paul visited do not know any of Jesus' followers in Jerusalem, but they knew the Jerusalem followers needed help. They also knew they were all brothers and sisters in Christ. God calls us to help other people when we can. We don't have to know people to be able to help them.

Prepare

- ✓ Provide copies of **Reproducible 5b: Paul's Third Missionary Journey**.
- ✓ If you have invited a visitor to come and read Paul's story to the class each week as suggested in Lesson 1, have this person tell the story.
- ✓ Supply Bibles.

Called to Give

Prepare

✓ Write the Bible verse on a marker board or a piece of mural paper and place it where it can easily be seen. ("God loves a cheerful giver." 2 Corinthians 9:7)

Prepare

✓ Invite someone in your church to visit the class and talk about ways your church helps people who are not in your church, either through giving money or giving goods and services.

✓ If you are not able to have a guest speaker, have the class brainstorm ways your church helps other people.

Grumpy or Cheerful Bible Verse

- **Say:** Our Bible verse today is from one of the letters Paul wrote to the believers at Corinth.

- Invite the children to read the Bible verse with you.

- **Ask:** What does it mean to be a cheerful giver? (wanting to give, giving willingly) What would it mean to be a grumpy giver? (feeling forced to give, giving unwillingly, being mad that you have to give)

- **Say:** Let's have some fun and say our Bible verse grumpily. Put on your grumpiest face and use your grumpiest voice.

- Encourage the children to read the Bible verse grumpily.

- **Say:** When Paul talked to people about giving, he reminded them where everything comes from. Everything we have is a gift from God. Paul told the people, "You've been blessed; now pass it on and give to others." That's a good reminder of why we give cheerfully. Let's say our verse one more time. This time, put on your most cheerful face and use your cheeriest voice.

- Encourage the children to read the verse cheerfully.

Called to Give

- **Say:** Just as the early churches gave to the offering for Jerusalem, our church also gives to help others. We have a guest today to talk about how our church helps people.

- Introduce your guest and invite them to tell the class about your church's missionary outreach.

- Encourage the children to be good listeners and ask questions.

- Thank your visitor for sharing with the class.

- **Say:** Choosing to follow Jesus means choosing to support God's work in our church and in other places too.

- Dismiss children to their small groups.

Small Groups

Divide the children into small groups. You may organize the groups around age levels or around readers and nonreaders. Keep the groups small, with a maximum of ten children in each group. You may need to have more than one group of each age level.

Young Children (Ages 5-7)

- **Say:** Paul asked the churches he visited to give offerings to help other people. Each person was encouraged to give what he or she could. We are called to give to help others too. We give what we can. Together our gifts can help many people. Our gifts aren't always money. There are many ways we can give to others.

- Give each child a piece of paper.

- **Say:** I am going to give each of you a card listing something you might give to someone else. Without showing anyone else your card, draw a picture showing someone giving the thing listed on your card.

- Give each child a card. Allow children time to draw pictures.

- Take turns guessing what each child has drawn. After each thing is guessed, discuss how giving that item or action could help someone else.

- **Ask:** Can you think of other things you have to offer that can help someone else?

- Allow children an opportunity to share their ideas.

- **Say:** Each of you has something to give to help other people. This is the way God's work gets done.

- **Pray:** God, thank you for the many blessings we have received. Help us look for ways we can do your work and help other people. Amen.

Prepare

- ✓ Write each of the following words on an index card or small piece of paper: *hug, flowers, drawing, sandwich, smile, toy, book, coat, shoes, money.*

- ✓ Supply paper and crayons.

Prepare

✓ Supply paper and pencils.

Older Children (Ages 8–11)

- **Ask:** Why was Paul encouraging the churches he visited to give money? (to help the believers in Jerusalem)

- **Say:** Paul encouraged each person to give what he or she was able to give. Not everyone gave the same amount. Those who had more gave more. We don't all have the same resources. We give what we are able to give. Together our gifts can help many people.

- Give each child a piece of paper and a pencil.

- **Say:** Giving money is one way to help others. There are many other ways each one of us can help do God's work.

- Have the children draw two lines to divide their paper into three sections.

- Have each child label the three sections with the following headings: "I can offer a prayer," "I can offer a donation," and "I can offer my time."

- **Say:** Think about whom you can pray for this week. Think about what you have to donate. It might be money. It might be something else to fill a need you know about. Think about what you can spend time doing this week that will help someone else.

- Allow children time to reflect and write.

- Invite the children to share their ideas with each other.

- **Say:** Not everyone came up with the same ideas, but each one of you has something to offer. This is the way God's work gets done.

- **Pray:** God, we bring what we have and offer it to you. Working together, we can do your work in the world. Help us always to be looking for ways to do your work. Amen.

Giving for God

As Paul traveled, he preached the good news. He also encouraged Jesus' followers to give offerings to help others. How much should each person give? Solve the puzzle to discover the answer.

1. In the grid below, cross out all words that are types of money.

2. Cross out all books of the Bible.

3. Write the remaining words, in order, on the lines below the grid.

dollar	Everyone	Acts	nickel	should	give
Philemon	dime	whatever	1 Corinthians	quarter	Ephesians
they	Romans	have	Galatians	decided	penny
in	Philippians	2 Corinthians	their	hearts	1 Thessalonians

_____

_____

Paul's Third Missionary Journey

Hello again! It's Paul, back to tell you about more of my experiences. After my second missionary journey, I had a chance to return to my home church at Antioch for a visit. It was good to see all my friends there and tell them about my journeys.

One thing about doing what the Holy Spirit tells you is that you never know for sure where you will be going or how long you will stay. While I was in Antioch, the Spirit let me know it was time to travel again. There were more places that needed the good news.

One of the places I visited was Ephesus. I spent two years there, preaching in the synagogue and the lecture hall. I knew God was helping me to spread the good news to all the Jews and Gentiles in the area, so I kept preaching every day. When I first arrived in Ephesus, they hadn't even heard of the Holy Spirit. I baptized some people in Jesus' name, and they received the Holy Spirit. While I was in Ephesus, God did amazing miracles through me. People even took handkerchiefs that I had touched to people who were sick, and those people were healed.

Some people in Ephesus had been worshiping other gods. I told them there is only one God. Many people made the decision to follow the one true God. Many good things were accomplished in Ephesus with God's help.

As I traveled and visited different churches I had helped to start on my previous journeys, I encouraged all the believers to donate to the offering for Jerusalem. As believers, we are committed to help one another. We are all one big family, even though we worship in different places. At the time, the believers in Jerusalem needed support.

I reminded those I visited that giving to others is best when it is done willingly and not grudgingly. I didn't tell them they had to give—it needed to be their decision. And there is no set amount for each person to give. Those with abundance should share with those who are in need. I also reminded the followers that God loves a cheerful or gracious giver.

(Based on Acts 19)

6 Called to Have Courage

<table>
<tr><td>

Objectives

The children will
- hear Acts 27–28.
- learn about Paul being shipwrecked on the island of Malta.
- discover that Paul's faith in God helped him have courage.
- explore how our faith can be a source of courage.

</td><td>

Bible Story

Paul's Shipwreck on Malta: Acts 27–28

Bible Verse

Stay awake, stand firm in your faith, be brave, be strong. (1 Corinthians 16:13)

</td></tr>
</table>

Focus for the Teacher

As a result of Paul's missionary efforts, many people became followers of Jesus. Paul's efforts were certainly important in the spread of Christianity. As we have already learned, Paul's journeys did not always go smoothly. He was imprisoned multiple times, and he needed courage to continue spreading the good news.

One of Paul's personal goals was to spread the good news in the city of Rome, but circumstances apparently prevented him from going there for some time. In Paul's letter to the Romans he writes, "I want you to know, brothers and sisters, that I planned to visit you many times, although I have been prevented from coming until now" (Romans 1:13). Eventually, however, Paul did set out for Rome—as a prisoner.

Paul had been imprisoned in Caesarea for some time awaiting trial when he was brought before Festus, the governor of Judea. Some of the chief priests and Jewish leaders had asked Festus to transfer Paul to Jerusalem, because they planned to attack Paul on the way and kill him. When Festus asked Paul if he was willing to travel to Jerusalem, Paul demanded that the emperor himself hold the trial. As a Roman citizen, Paul had

> Paul needed courage to continue spreading the good news.

the right to appeal his case to the emperor. Those were the circumstances that led to Paul being transported to Rome as a prisoner. However, Paul was not destined for smooth sailing.

The ship Paul was on was delayed by poor wind conditions. At one point Paul warned the captain that it was not safe to sail, and if they proceeded their ship and cargo would be badly damaged (Acts 27:10). Although this sounds like a prophecy, it was not meant to be; Paul was speaking not as a prophet but as an experienced sailor. Paul's advice was ignored, however, and the ship sailed on.

Eventually the ship encountered hurricane-force winds and was in such danger of sinking that the crew began to throw cargo overboard in an attempt to lighten the ship. After several days of battling the fierce storm, the crew gave up all hope of being saved.

Paul, on the other hand, knew God intended him to reach Rome in order to help spread the good news there. He reported to the crew and other passengers that he had been visited by an angel, who assured him the lives of everyone on the ship would be saved. Paul not only was brave, but he encouraged those around him so they were brave also!

56

Explore Interest Groups

Be sure that adult leaders are waiting when the first child arrives. Greet and welcome the children. Get them involved in an activity that interests them and introduces the theme for the day's activities.

Paint a Stormy Sea

- **Say:** We've been talking about the missionary journeys the Apostle Paul took. In today's story, we will hear about a time that Paul was on a ship when a terrible storm occurred.

- **Ask:** What does the sky look like during a bad storm? What does the water look like during a bad storm?

- Give each child a piece of paper.

- Show the children how to use their brushes to add water to the watercolor paint and stir to make paint.

- Invite each child to paint a picture of a stormy sea.

- **Ask:** What happens to boats that are on the water during a storm? (They get tossed about.)

- Have each child cut a boat shape out of brown construction paper and a sail shape out of white paper.

- Encourage each child to glue the boat and sail on the stormy sea picture.

Prepare

- ✓ Provide watercolor paints, paintbrushes, white paper, brown construction paper, scissors, glue, table covering or newspaper, paint smocks, and empty plastic containers.

- ✓ Cover the work area with protective covering or newspaper. Have the children wear smocks to protect their clothing.

- ✓ Fill plastic containers half full of water.

The Comfort Zone

- Have the children stand inside the circle of chairs.

- **Say:** It takes courage to share the good news with other people as Paul did. Paul was able to do this because he knew God was with him everywhere he went. We may not be comfortable telling others about God. When we do something we are not comfortable with, we call that "going outside of our comfort zone." We are going to play a game called "The Comfort Zone." The area inside this circle of chairs is the comfort zone. I am going to read some situations to you. If you would be comfortable in the situation, stay inside the circle of chairs. If the situation would be difficult or make you uncomfortable, step outside the circle of chairs.

- Read the following situations to the children and let them move in and out of the circle:

  o Telling someone that I go to church.
  o Inviting someone to come to church with me.
  o Asking someone if he or she believes in Jesus.
  o Telling my family about a story from the Bible.
  o Telling a friend about a story from the Bible.
  o Going to church with someone else.

Prepare

- ✓ Place chairs in a circle, leaving enough space among the chairs for children to go in and out of the circle.

o Telling my family that God loves them.
o Telling someone at church that God loves him or her.
o Telling someone at school that God loves him or her.

- **Say:** We may not feel completely comfortable sharing the good news with other people. However, we know that God will be with us and will help us have courage when we need to step outside our comfort zone.

The Paul Wall

- **Say:** Today is our last week of studying Paul. We have learned a lot about Paul in the last few weeks.

- Invite each child to draw or write something they know about Paul on the mural paper.

- If children have difficulty deciding what to draw, remind them of the stories they have heard about Paul losing his sight on the road to Damascus, traveling to spread the good news, being thrown in prison, writing letters, and collecting an offering for Jerusalem.

Let's Review

- **Say:** Today is the last lesson in our study of Paul. Let's review what we've learned.

- Give each child a pencil and a copy of Reproducible 6a: Paul Word Find.

- Encourage the children to work individually or together to complete the word find.

Prepare

✓ Cut a large piece of mural paper and hang it where the children will be able to write and draw on it.

✓ Supply crayons.

Prepare

✓ Provide copies of **Reproducible 6a: Paul Word Find**.

✓ Supply pencils.

Answer Key

O	F	F	E	R	I	N	G	W	P	L
S	P	B	E	V	O	L	U	A	S	D
W	L	E	T	T	E	R	S	N	U	M
E	C	L	N	P	J	E	A	B	C	A
N	O	I	O	R	K	I	P	A	S	P
D	R	E	P	I	T	A	U	R	A	O
O	I	V	U	S	L	P	L	N	M	S
O	N	E	I	O	I	A	L	A	A	T
G	T	R	U	N	L	L	P	B	D	L
A	H	J	E	S	U	S	A	A	U	E
C	E	V	I	G	O	D	L	S	P	A
M	I	S	S	I	O	N	A	R	Y	U

58   *The Call: Children's Leader Guide*

Large Group

Bring all the children together to experience the Bible story. Use a bell to alert the children to the large-group time.

Make a Storm

- Have the children stand up and face you.

- **Say:** Today we will hear a story of Paul getting caught in a storm at sea. Right now we are going to use our bodies to make it sound like there is a rainstorm in our room. Listen for my directions and follow my actions.

- Give the following directions, demonstrating the actions as you describe them. Allow a few moments between each direction.

  o The rain begins very softly. Gently rub your hands together in a circular motion.
  o After awhile it begins raining harder. Rub your hands together harder and faster.
  o Rub your hands together harder.
  o Snap your fingers.
  o Then the rain begins to pour down. Pat your thighs with your hands.
  o There is thunder! Jump in place three times. Remember to continue patting your thighs.
  o After awhile the storm begins to slow down. Snap your fingers.
  o Rub your hands together quickly in a circular motion.
  o Gently rub your hands together.
  o Place your hands at your side.

- Have the children sit down.

Paul's Shipwreck on Malta

- **Say:** Today we will hear one more story about Paul.

- **Ask:** Which book of the Bible have our stories come from during this study? (Acts) Is Acts in the Old Testament or the New Testament? (New Testament)

- Encourage the children to find Acts in their Bibles.

- Read the Bible story from Reproducible 6b: Paul's Shipwreck on Malta.

- **Ask:** Why did Paul have faith that they would all survive the shipwreck? (God sent an angel to tell him he would make it to Rome.) What did Paul do that took courage? (He survived the shipwreck and gave encouragement to the other people on the boat.)

- **Say:** Paul not only had courage himself, but he was able to help the rest of the people have courage too.

Prepare

✓ Provide copies of **Reproducible 6b: Paul's Shipwreck on Malta**.

✓ If you have invited a visitor to come and read Paul's story to the class each week as suggested in Lesson 1, have them tell the story.

✓ Supply Bibles.

Called to Have Courage

Prepare

✓ Write the Bible verse on a marker board or a piece of mural paper, and place it where it can easily be seen. ("Stay awake, stand firm in your faith, be brave, be strong." 1 Corinthians 16:13)

✓ *Optional*: If you have a large class, divide the children into eleven sections and have one section stand up as each word as said.

Bible Verse Wave

- Have the children sit in a circle.

- **Say:** Today's Bible verse is from a letter Paul wrote to believers in Corinth.

- Invite the children to read the Bible verse with you.

- **Ask:** When did Paul need to be brave? (when he was thrown in prison; when he was shipwrecked)

- **Say:** Now we are going to make things more challenging by adding the wave as we say the Bible verse.

- Choose one child to begin the wave.

- **Say:** We will say the Bible verse together. As we say the first word, the first person will stand up and raise both arms in the air and then sit down. As we say the second word, the person to the right will stand up with arms in the air and sit down. The wave will continue around the circle as we say the verse with one person standing for each word we say.

- Have all the children say the Bible verse as the wave travels around the circle.

- Repeat the activity several times, challenging the children to get faster with each attempt.

Called to Have Courage

- **Say:** We can learn a lot from the Apostle Paul. Paul taught a lot of people about Jesus. It took courage to keep spreading the good news when it became difficult. We are going to join together in what is called a litany. I will read some statements about Paul. Your response is "If Paul can do it, so can we!"

- Have the children practice their response.

- Lead the children in the following litany:

  o **Leader:** Paul changed his heart and became a follower of Jesus.
  o Children: If Paul can do it, so can we!
  o **Leader:** Everywhere he went, Paul spread the good news and told people about Jesus.
  o Children: If Paul can do it, so can we!
  o **Leader:** Paul was faithful to God, even when life was difficult.
  o Children: If Paul can do it, so can we!
  o **Leader:** Paul's actions reflected God's love.
  o Children: If Paul can do it, so can we!
  o **Leader:** Paul cheerfully shared what he had with those in need.
  o Children: If Paul can do it, so can we!
  o **Leader:** Paul's faith in God gave him the courage to continue to spread the good news.
  o Children: If Paul can do it, so can we!

- Dismiss children to their small groups.

Small Groups

Divide the children into small groups. You may organize the groups around age levels or around readers and nonreaders. Keep the groups small, with a maximum of ten children in each group. You may need to have more than one group of each age level.

Young and Older Children

- **Say:** We've learned a lot about Paul. Remember that before Paul met Jesus on the road to Damascus, he was involved in persecuting believers. Paul's life is an example of how God can change people's hearts and use them to do God's work. Let's take a look at what we've learned about Paul and see how we can follow his example.

- Give each child a pencil and a copy of Reproducible 6c: Paul's Call and My Call.

- Use the following questions as a guide for discussing the table. Encourage older children to write their answers to the questions in the "Me" column.

  - Called to Follow Christ: When did you begin following Jesus? Because you follow Jesus, how is your life different from what it would be if you were not a follower?
  - Called to Go: What are the places you go? Who can you tell about Jesus?
  - Called to Be Faithful: What helps you remember God is with you when life is hard? Who can you turn to for help when you need it?
  - Called to Love: Who shows God's love to you? What are some ways you show God's love to others?
  - Called to Give: What are some ways you give money to help others? What are some different things you can give to help those in need?
  - Called to Have Courage: Has there been a time when it has been hard to remember God is with you? How might you step out of your comfort zone to spread the good news?

- **Say:** Paul took a lot of journeys to spread the good news. He must have gotten tired sometimes, but he continued to do God's work. We are also on a journey to do God's work. We can look for ways to love and serve others and to spread the good news wherever we are.

- **Pray:** God, thank you for stories of Paul that help us learn how to be better followers of Jesus. Give us the courage to share your love with everyone we meet. Amen.

Prepare

- ✓ *Note:* Although younger and older children are doing the same activities in their small groups this week, the level of discussion will vary according to the age of children in each group. With younger children, discuss the questions and have them talk about their answers rather than filling out the table.

- ✓ Provide copies of **Reproducible 6c: Paul's Call and My Call**.

- ✓ Supply pencils.

Paul Word Find

Find the underlined words in the puzzle. Words may be forward, backward, up, down, or diagonal.

Paul was an apostle, someone sent by Jesus to teach others about God.

Before Paul believed in Jesus and became an apostle, he persecuted Christians.

Paul's Hebrew name was Saul.

Paul did not become a believer until after Jesus' resurrection.

On the road to Damascus, Paul had an encounter with the risen Jesus that changed his life.

Paul and his friend Barnabas were the first missionaries.

Paul spread the good news wherever he went.

As he traveled on his missionary journeys, Paul started many new churches.

When he was away from the churches he started, Paul wrote letters to them, encouraging and instructing them in their ministry.

Paul and Silas were thrown into prison for casting a spirit out of a slave girl.

When the Christians at Corinth began to argue, Paul wrote and reminded them to treat each other with love.

O	F	F	E	R	I	N	G	W	P	L
S	P	B	E	V	O	L	U	A	S	D
W	L	E	T	T	E	R	S	N	U	M
E	C	L	N	P	J	E	A	B	C	A
N	O	I	O	R	K	I	P	A	S	P
D	R	E	P	I	T	A	A	R	A	O
O	I	V	U	S	L	P	U	N	M	S
O	N	E	I	O	I	A	L	A	A	T
G	T	R	U	N	L	L	P	B	D	L
A	H	J	E	S	U	S	A	A	U	E
C	E	V	I	G	O	D	L	S	P	A
M	I	S	S	I	O	N	A	R	Y	U

Paul's Shipwreck on Malta

It's Paul here, to tell you one more story. It's the story of my journey to Rome. For a long time I had wanted to visit Rome, but it didn't seem to work out. Then I was put in prison because some priests and Jewish leaders were not happy with my missionary work. Being in prison is never a good thing, but in this case it did allow me to go to Rome. I was sent to Rome so the emperor of the Roman Empire could hear the case against me. However, the journey to Rome didn't go as planned.

After the ship sailed, we had delays and weren't able to travel as quickly as the crew had hoped. The weather was getting bad. Having experience as a sailor, I warned the ship's captain and crew that if they continued to travel, there would be damage to the ship and some people might lose their lives.

I guess it's not surprising that they didn't listen to me, since I was a prisoner. The captain decided to sail on anyway. Pretty soon we encountered a fierce storm with strong winds. After several days, the ship had been so battered by the storm that the crew began to throw cargo overboard to lighten the load so the ship wouldn't fall apart. After a few more days, when the storm was still going strong, the crew gave up hope that any of them would live through the storm.

I had faith we would survive. An angel from God had visited me and told me I would make it to Rome because God had work for me there. I encouraged the crew and passengers to have courage and not give up! I guess they were desperate, because this time they listened to me. I told them we would all be saved but they needed to run aground on an island because the ship was not going to make it.

Eventually the ship did come to an island called Malta. The ship fell apart but the entire crew and all the passengers, including me, were able to swim to the island and be saved. We had to spend a few months on Malta, but eventually we were able to find another ship and travel on to Rome.

I've shared many of my experiences with you the last few weeks. Lots of unexpected things happened to me. Life is like that—you are never quite sure what will come next. My faith in God gave me the courage to face whatever happened.

(Based on Acts 27–28)

Paul's Call and My Call

	Paul	Me
Called to Follow Christ	Paul had an encounter on the road to Damascus that changed his life. He became a follower of Jesus.	
Called to Go	Paul was a missionary. He traveled to many places. Everywhere he went, he told people about Jesus.	
Called to Be Faithful	Paul continued to follow Jesus even when life was difficult. He continued to spread the good news.	
Called to Love	Paul reminded people that God loves us, and we pass that love on to others. Love is the greatest thing.	
Called to Give	Paul encouraged believers to give cheerfully to help and support each other.	
Called to Have Courage	Paul's faith helped him face difficult tasks with courage. Paul remembered God was always with him.	